Purpose of the book:

This book is an update of my original 8D book published in 2013. The "Instructive Example" part is basically unchanged other than a few corrections.

There are several new appendices added to cover greater detail in how to effect some of the steps. These are:

Obtain management support

Use the team approach

Methodology to develop potential root causes

Verification of effectiveness of the corrective actions.

In this example we are looking at our imaginary firm named MCP Industries. MCP is a direct supplier to Strand Industries, a major OEM. Strand has experienced a quality issue with our product. The complaint is that a small gear mechanism has a rusty output pin. A rejection has been issued against MCP Industries and they have submitted a preliminary 8D based on early investigation of the issue. In this example, MCP Industries has now prepared a full 8D to give to their customer.

This example is intended to be used as a teaching tool for improvement in the elements of 8D problem solving methodology.

There are 8 disciplines in structured problem solving (Thus the term "8D.") In this book, a realistic example is given of each discipline. A section titled "Comments" follows teach example. The comments represent clarification of what is required and it also tells what is unacceptable because certain common actions actually do not contribute to problem solving. These are the "Do's and Don'ts" which are necessary to write a good problem solving report.

Problem solving teams must have a well defined leader. This is a person who will keep the team on track and encourage positive teamwork. A good leader will work the team through the 8D steps and ensure that each step is completed correctly.

It is highly recommended that problem solving teams have additional training on the skills used in problem solving such as SPC, Capability analysis, Sampling – including sample error, Comparison of attribute vs. variables data, measurement error, etc. Without common understanding of these topics, the team may work at cross-purposes.

The table below shows the format for the example within this book. Each of the eight disciplines are discussed in the following order:

Explanation of format for discussing the 8-Disciplines

1. Identification of the specific discipline under discussion
2. An example of the particular step of the 8D
3. Guidance, comments and "Do's and "Don'ts

Each "Discipline" within the 8D process is discussed using a 2-section format as outlined below.

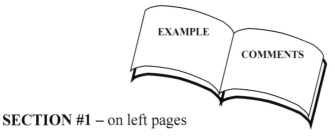

EXAMPLE

COMMENTS

SECTION #1 – on left pages

Presentation of an example which is intended to be a realistic situation. In this case, all examples are relating to a problem which was indentified by our customer. The resulting rejection of an incoming shipment was our first awareness of the issue.

SECTION #2 – on right pages

A listing of *DO's and DON'T's* for each discipline. Also included are helpful comments. This is a very important section and it is aimed at focusing on finding and correcting the root cause of the problem. Special attention is needed to prevent the team from looking making mistakes such as:

1. Erroneously listing symptoms as root causes
2. Failing to fix the root cause (i.e. adding another inspection for example).
3. Neglecting the need to correct the system root cause (i.e. what within the system permitted the root cause to happen and, once it happened, why did it escape our detection?)
4. Seeking to blame others for the problem.

TABLE OF CONTENTS

APPENDICES

#1 EXAMPLE - USE THE TEAM APPROACH

MCP Industries Personnel:

Bill Smith – Champion, Plant Manager
Don Simpson – Engineering Supervisor
Fred Russell – Receiving Inspector
Dave Brill – Grinder Operator – EI Team Leader
Mary Clark – QC Manager
George Jones – Mfg. Superintendent

Sub-Supplier Personnel:

John Brown – QC Manager, Ace Heat Treating
Bob Gardner – Tech Rep – Hi-Tek Coolants
Ann Bowen – Tech. Rep. Fab Steel Co.

Strand Industries Personnel:

Larry James - Strand Ind. Process Engineer
Bill Thompson – Product Design Engineer

#1 C O M M E N T S

CHAMPION:

He/She provides the resources and the climate for problem solving. Also, he/she secures management support for team member involvement. (See Appendix IV for a discussion of management support)

TEAM FORMATION:

Consider all affected activities

> Sub Suppliers of components
> Raw Material Sources
> Purchased services sources
> Customer
> Machine Builder
> Gage and/or test equipment supplier
> Inside/Outside experts
> Packaging Engineers
> Others

The magnitude of the problem may dictate the depth of the brainstorming phase.

Obtain the "Buy-in" of each participating activity.

GOALS – Define the 8D team goals in writing as an initial team activity. Obtain group consensus.

RULES – Clearly define the team rules.

> #1 – NO CRITICISM – Everyone's opinion is important

> #2 – EVERYONE CONTRIBUTES – it is ok to "pass," but each team member must participate.

See Appendix V for a detailed discussion of what is involved in the Team Approach.

#2   EXAMPLE - DESCRIBE THE PROBLEM

RUSTY OUTPUT GEAR STATIONARY PIN

On 3/17/16, The Strand Industries Main Plant rejected 17,290 pcs of output gear pins for the presence of rust. The engineering drawing requires the parts to be rust-free. A sample of 50 output gear pins revealed 17 rusty parts, or 34% defective.

#2 C O M M E N T S

This section must be stated in the customer's terms.

Dates must be stated – start date/end date, including production date of production lots with defective parts.

Frequency and trends in percent defective must be documented

Other quantification includes:

Actual measurements and statistical capability (process potential) estimates.

State clearly what present requirements exist. *This includes specifications, process checks and controls, standards and other agreements*

5W2H: Who, What, Where, When, Why, How, and How Many. It is a good practice to ask "Why" at least 5 times. *Ask "Why until it does not make sense to drill down any deeper.*

Obtain and use specifications, process flow diagrams or other schematics, which show requirements, process, inspection, travel, storage, etc.

Use minimal basic descriptions (i.e.: Rusty output gear pins) and then give a short explanatory paragraph.

Avoid the common mistake of characterizing the problem as follows:

"The Strand Industries Main Plant found rusty output gear pins......"

The problem is that "We" made the defect, not that the customer found it.

#3 E X A M P L E – CONTAINMENT AND SHORT TERM CORRECTIVE ACTIONS

3/17/16 - All available stock was isolated and sorted with the following results:

Location	Pcs Sorted	Pcs Rejected	Percent Rejected	Confidence
Main Plant	17,290	7,123	41%	95%
Acme	96,500	8,974	9%	95%
HT Treat	38,000	1,486	4%	95%
TOTALS	151,790	17,583	12%	

3/18/16 – Sort Completion (System Purged)

Other Short Term Corrective Actions:

3/18/16 – Added 100% visual inspection at pack line – est. 95% effective.

3/18/16 – Conducted a process audit. Result – All processing parameters were judged to be acceptable to existing process standard.

3/19/16 – Reviewed all raw material in inventory for presence of (a) Undersize, (b) Excess Rust and/or pitting. NONE FOUND

3/19/16 – Reviewed the problem with the Employee Involvement (EI) group and involved the EI group in a team brainstorming activity

#3 COMMENTS

It is not necessary to know root cause at this initial time. The first objective is to protect the customer from experiencing any additional defective stock

Containment actions must extend to:

Your operations

Your warehouse

Repair/rework Area

In-transit stock: *That which is in-transit to and from customer and all sub-suppliers, platers, heat treaters, component sources, finishers, etc.*

What is the % effectiveness of your containment? How was it determined?

List any other short term actions the team has taken (These may be actions taken prior to determining root cause)

What were the dates of the containment actions?

What was found – (this should be quantified)

Audits are not acceptable as containment ACTIONS.

Key Words:

DATA
DATES
QUANTIFICATION
VERIFICATION

#4a   E X A M P L E – DEFINE & VERIFY ROOT CAUSE

A Team brainstorming session of 3/17/16 resulted in identification of 3 potential process root causes and 3 potential system root causes as indicated below. (See appendix VI for a description of how to direct the team to develop the root causes)

PROCESS ROOT CAUSES:

Priority	Potential Process Root Cause	Estimated % Contribution
1	New Cardboard Dunnage Separators used by Fab Metal Treating Co. have acid residue, that attacks steel.	75%
2	Coolant supplied by Hi-Tek and coolants used by Fab Metal Treating Co. do not inhibit rust.	25%
3	Stock O.D. Size from Fab Steel Co. is not sufficient to allow for "clean-up" during the rough and final grinding operations.	5%

SYSTEM ROOT CAUSES:

Priority	Potential Process Root Cause	Estimated % Contribution
1	Failure to prove-out a process change	75%

#4a C O M M E N T S

The brainstorming team should have copies of the Fishbone Diagram and the Is/Is-Not analysis on the wall for all to consider in their discussions. These two documents are very helpful in identifying potential root causes. See Appendix I and II for the Fishbone Diagram and the is/is-not analysis.

Keep asking Why, Why, Why?

As we explore each new "Why", we approach closer to the true root cause. We should stop asking "Why" when we begin to consider root causes which are clearly beyond our control (i.e.: Weather, Atmosphere, etc)

Challenge each Root Cause as a symptom or an effect.

Recognize that there is usually a PROCESS root cause and a SYSTEM root cause.

PROCESS root cause: The immediate cause, which acts directly on the manufacturing system.

SYSTEM Root cause: The underlying cause which is within the management system and permits the conditions to exist which result in the process root cause.

The team should jointly determine (or estimate) the contribution of each potential root cause. (See right-hand column in table on prior page)

A fishbone analysis should be considered MANDATORY (This is also referred to as an Ishikawa diagram). See Appendix I for an example.

Is/is-not analysis similarly should be considered MANDATORY. See Appendix II for an example.

#4b. EXAMPLE - DEFINE & VERIFY ROOT CAUSE

VERIFICATION OF ROOT CAUSE:

Cause Ident.	Date	Verification Action	Estimate% Confidence.
P-1	3/18/16	Inspection of the rust pattern on the rejected parts revealed "line" pattern of rust that indicates contact with cardboard separator surfaces	99+%
P-2	3/18/16	A lab chip test using in-process coolant developed rust on chips after 36 hours. The rust protection for this product is 48 hours with no red rust. Additionally, the coolant pH was 6.8 vs. the tech data sheet requires the pH be maintained at 7.1 to 7.3.	100%
P-3	3/19/16	A tolerance stack-up study indicated that minimum stock diameter when coupled with maximum finished output pin diameter, developed the potential for "no clean-up" if pitting or scale is deeper than .002"	25%

#4b C O M M E N T S –(Included in #4a comments.)

For purposes of identifying the category of root cause, the left side of the following examples have codes such as P-1, P-2, S-1, etc. This is to highlight the categorization of the root to "Process" or to "System." As added root causes are considered, they are numbered sequentially within each category. Also, beneath these codes there is a label such as "Prevention" or "Detection." This is identification of the corrective actions as either working on preventing the concern or merely detecting it. Prevention actions can significantly lower costs while Detection actions keep a lot of non-value added costs within the process.

#5/6a. EXAMPLE – IMPLEMENT AND VERIFY PERMANENT CORRECTIVE ACTIONS

VERIFICATION OF
PERMANENT CORRECTIVE ACTIONS:

Cause Ident.	Date	Corrective Actions	Estimate % Confidence
P-1 (Prevention)	3/20/16	Resin coated white cardboard was reinstated in production. These are the same separators as used prior to the problem. This material has been added to the process sheets and specified on the bill of materials.	99+%
P-2 (Prevention)	3/20/16	The in-process coolant will be monitored daily for pH and adjusted or discarded when it drops below pH 7.1. The PFMEA has been changed to reflect the pH controls.	99+%
P-3 (Prevention)	3/24/16	All bar material was re-specified to be purchased at .003" larger stock diameter.	100%
S-1 (Prevention)	3/20/16	The Fab Ht Treat Co. procedures were modified to require prove-out of all significant process changes	95%
S-2 (System)	3/26/16	The characteristic of "rust" has been added to the dock audit instruction sheet. The results will be logged in the Dock Audit record sheet	95%
S-3 (System)	4/1/16	FMEA Updated	100%

#5/6a C O M M E N T S

Label each action to identify the PROCESS or SYSTEM root cause it is acting on (This permits an "accounting" system to ensure each cause has an action directed toward it)

Identify whether each action is PREVENTION or DETECTION. (The best and lowest cost solution involves the use of preventive actions)

QOS reporting systems are an excellent source of verification data. Also use SPC charts, Cpk's, Ppk's, before and after the fix. ("...the Cpk was 0.53 prior to the fix and 1.8 after the corrective action – studies attached as back-up)
Another example: "Prior to actions, throughput losses were 1.36%. After the 3/11/16 fix, the process throughput losses were 0.04% - as per attached Percent defective (Rust) chart."

DO NOT rely on your customer for verification !. (i.e.: Avoid statements like the following: "The Strand Industries Main Plant receiving inspection has not reject any more shipments.")

Is the timing, frequency, and % defective consistent with the stated root cause?

We would expect to see the customer data in the Paynter chart as a part of the verification, but it should only supplement other data (i.e.: see above DO NOT rely on your customer for verification)

#5/6b. EXAMPLE – IMPLEMENT AND VERIFY
PERMANENT CORRECTIVE ACTIONS

VERIFICATION OF CORRECTIVE ACTIONS

Paynter Chart
Showing Percent Defective (Rust) by Date with Pareto Chart

		D A T E				
Location	3/5	3/12	3/19	3/26	4/2	4/9
FAB HT	N/A	41%	21%	0%	0%	0%
Strand Ind.	0%	1.2%	3.7%	0%	0%	0%

Note: Containment actions implemented 3/22/16

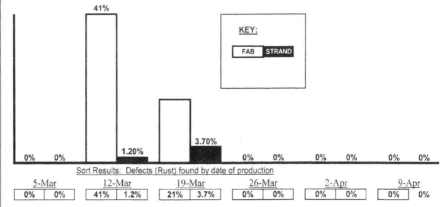

Note: Containment actions implemented 3/22/16

#5/6b COMMENTS

A Paynter chart is an effective display of data for the purpose of convincing your customer that containment and permanent corrective actions have been implemented. A Paynter Chart is simply a run chart with a Pareto Chart.

To illustrate a few actions directed toward root cause, consider an additional example in which the defect is **breakage of plastic snap tabs** on a plastic part, due to excessive stress.

Potential types of actions directed toward the true root cause:

    A. Eliminate the Root Cause (i.e.: "tabs break" – redesign to eliminate stress by moving the tabs to other areas

    B. Do an "end run" on the root cause. (i.e.: Eliminate tabs)

    C. Design for robustness (i.e.: make tabs bigger, stronger, better stress loading, compliance, etc)

Actions toward the System Root Cause:

    A. Update the DV plan to find this condition when it is under development.

    B. Update the process sheets to include a check for broken tabs

    C. Revise the DVP&R to include a requirement for tab robustness.

Other considerations:

    Once actions are recommended ask the team the following questions:

- Do these actions make sense when reviewing the root causes listed in section #4?
- Do these actions adequately cover the location, timing, and magnitude as listed in the problem statement?

#7   EXAMPLE - PREVENT RECURRENCE

3/20/16– The PFMEA was revised to add
RUST as a concern with the following
RPN Weights

$$
\begin{array}{ll}
\text{SEVERITY} = & 6 \\
\text{DETECTION} = & 5 \\
\underline{\text{OCCURRENCE} =} & \underline{5} \\
\text{RPN} = 150\ (6\text{x}5\text{x}5)
\end{array}
$$

As noted above, permanent preventive actions were implemented on
each of the process and system root causes.

#7 COMMENTS

Be sure to explore all necessary modifications to the management system as well as the operating systems

Also consider all necessary modifications to practices and procedures.

The actions must be directed toward the Root Cause(s)

IMPORTANT – THE FOLLOWING ITEMS ARE NOT ALLOWED AS PREVENTIVE ACTIONS:

    Detection Actions

    Audits

    Inspections

#8. EXAMPLE - RECOGNIZE THE TEAM

This could be anything from a short note of closure to a formal note in someone's personnel file recognizing both the individual's contribution and the spirit of the team approach.

For people outside of your immediate organization, this could be a business luncheon or if the contribution was "above and beyond," it could be notes to people's immediate supervisors.

The level of recognition should vary with the importance of the corrective actions on the organization. (ie: Monetary, reputation, maintaining existing customers, potential for growth, etc.)

#8 C O M M E N T S

Recognize the team effort.

Recognize the individual contributions

Document the efforts

Add the lessons learned to the organization knowledge base:

Significant/Critical Characteristics

PFMEA
    Process Sheets
    Design Guides
    FMEA
    Maintenance requirements
    Other…

Report to Management

Appendix I – Fishbone Diagram Example

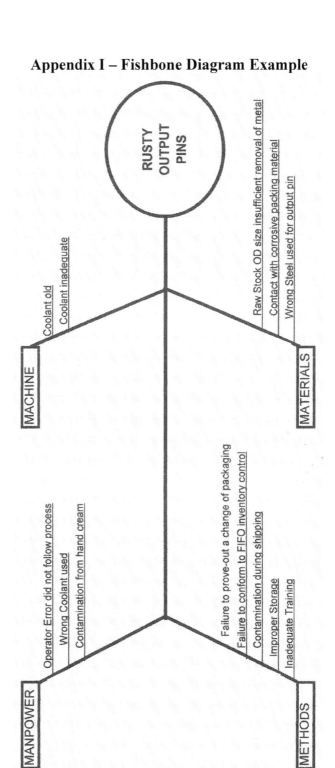

RUSTY OUTPUT PINS

MACHINE
- Coolant old
- Coolant inadequate

MATERIALS
- Raw Stock OD size insufficient removal of metal
- Contact with corrosive packing material
- Wrong Steel used for output pin

MANPOWER
- Operator Error did not follow process
- Wrong Coolant used
- Contamination from hand cream

METHODS
- Failure to prove-out a change of packaging
- Failure to conform to FIFO inventory control
- Contamination during shipping
- Improper Storage
- Inadequate Training

Appendix I – Comments on the Fishbone Diagram Example

The following illustration depicts the output of a team brainstorming effort as described in the section titled "#4a – DEFINE & VERIFY ROOT CAUSE.

As early as possible after team formation, the team leader should conduct a brainstorming session. During the brainstorming, the team leader presents an empty diagram with the problem in the circle and the "4M's" are already in the diagram: Manpower, Machine, Methods, and Materials. As an option, the team leader can suggest other general areas to include in the boxed areas of this diagram. Other areas such as Environment etc. could be added if the team felt it were necessary to facilitate brainstorming.

This session usually takes 1 to 2 hours to complete. It is most effective when knowledgeable people from all departments and areas which could have input in either correcting or verifying the problem under review. It is mandatory that group leader establish a relaxed climate free of fear of speaking out. The two most important rules are (1) Everyone contributes, even if it is a verbal "Pass," or "I don't know." and (2) No criticism. While it is ok to challenge input if you have added knowledge, but do not allow personal attacks or general negative statements.

All ideas should be put on the Fishbone diagram. After development of the Fishbone Diagram, the next step is to prioritize these POTENTIAL root causes.

Appendix II – Is/Is-Not Analysis

Rusty Output Pin		
IS	IS NOT	MAY BE
First observed 3/17/16 by Customer	Observed before 3/17/16	May have existed undetected in past
12% defective	100% defective	Other defect rates
	Found in Main Plant	Due to storage or transit
	Not a raw material issue	Packaging (new cardboard)
		Stock ID size (insufficient metal removal)
		Coolants - insufficient rust inhibitor

Appendix II – Comments on the Is/Is-Not Analysis

This is an optional exercise and it can be extremely useful. This is usually prepared by 1 or 2 individuals who have the most knowledge of the specific issue being investigated.

The Is/Is-Not Analysis should be completed before the brainstorming session and either displayed for the team to see or else given to team members as a handout.

The first 5-10 minutes of the brainstorming session should be devoted to a review and revision of the Is/Is-not analysis when all the team members can give their inputs.

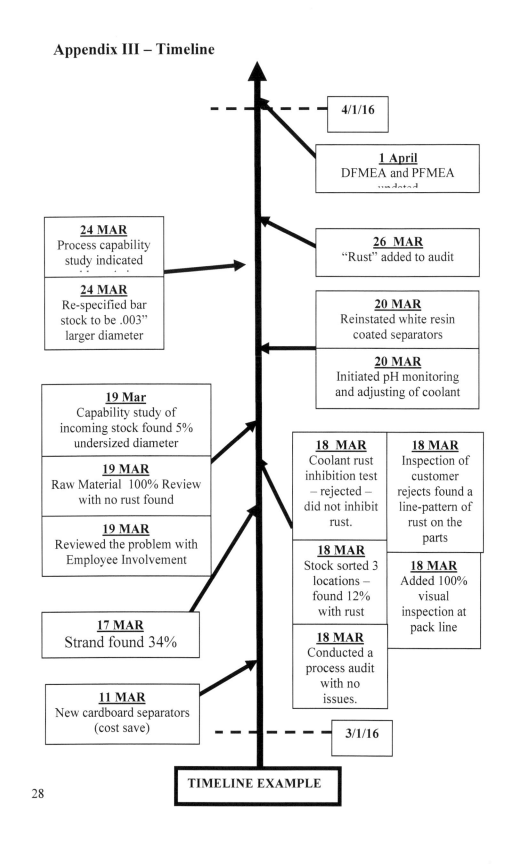

4/1/16

1 April
DFMEA and PFMEA
updated

24 MAR
Process capability
study indicated

26 MAR
"Rust" added to audit

24 MAR
Re-specified bar
stock to be .003"
larger diameter

20 MAR
Reinstated white resin
coated separators

20 MAR
Initiated pH monitoring
and adjusting of coolant

19 Mar
Capability study of
incoming stock found 5%
undersized diameter

19 MAR
Raw Material 100% Review
with no rust found

19 MAR
Reviewed the problem with
Employee Involvement

18 MAR
Coolant rust
inhibition test
– rejected –
did not inhibit
rust.

18 MAR
Inspection of
customer
rejects found a
line-pattern of
rust on the
parts

18 MAR
Stock sorted 3
locations –
found 12%
with rust

18 MAR
Added 100%
visual
inspection at
pack line

17 MAR
Strand found 34%

18 MAR
Conducted a
process audit
with no
issues.

11 MAR
New cardboard separators
(cost save)

3/1/16

TIMELINE EXAMPLE

Appendix III (cont'd) – Comments on the Timeline

Similar to the Is/Is-Not Analysis, the Timeline analysis can also be extremely useful, especially for complicated issues.

Again, his is usually prepared by 1 or 2 individuals who have the most knowledge of the specific issue being investigated.

Also, the Timeline should either be displayed or handed to the team members on a printed form. The review and revision of the Timeline should be conducted at the same time as the review of the Is/Is-Not analysis.

Appendix IV: Obtain Management Support

The assumption is that upper management in each organization whole-heartedly supports the idea of problem solving. In fact, they typically give rewards to people who they perceive to be solving the problems of the company. I will go out on a limb here and say that 90% of upper management really pays lip service to the idea of solving problems. Once the "Fix" has been declared and the internal or external customers are apparently satisfied, the issue is considered to be behind us. When the same problem reappears, the very same team "fixes" it again, possibly with the same woefully inadequate actions as per the previous times. *(Example: How many times have your problems been fixed with the old standby, "Retrain the operators?")*

If your management expects the cause to be found and the fix to be magically implemented, it is time to enlighten your managers or else move to a different company where competitive forces demand discipline in problem solving. Solving any complex problem requires that those individuals whose activities are impacted, including those who may be outside your company if applicable, commit to a few days of focused attention on problem solving and action planning.

If you are involved in problem solving either as a team leader or a team member, stand your ground and insist that management demonstrates their commitment to resolution by providing the time and resources for a team approach. EMPHASIS: The management should kick off the team meeting by stating their support. If they are too busy or feel that "It should be obvious" that they support the effort, it is a red flag which can doom the effort if management is not willing to give open, unqualified support for solving the problem.

Management support should clearly include stating support for finding the potential root causes, establishing plans to determine the true root causes, and developing action plans for both process root causes and system root causes. In addition, management should clearly be willing to allocate both the time and resources necessary for the problem solving team to accomplish its goals.

Appendix V – Use the Team Approach

Upper management should openly commit to supporting the team. This is most important and is discussed in the previous chapter.

Management should choose the team leader. The team leader should have input into the make-up of the team. As an example, if a person who is habitually inattentive, negative or disruptive is suggested, he/she may be ruled out if it is in the best interest of team dynamics. In some cases, however, disruptive individuals can turn out to be the highest contributors if you can find out why they are behaving in that manner and then harness their energy toward the team goals.

A conference room must be set aside for the problem solving team. It is very important to remove the individuals from the environment of their day-to-day job. This could be on-site but an off-site conference room is highly recommended for this important task. Participants must have management support to ensure that someone can fill in their duties and protect them from receiving text messages and cell phone calls. The facilitator must emphasize the no calls or texts rule at the start of the meetings. Mid-morning and mid-afternoon breaks are the time to deal with these types of communications. Distractions will diminish the team effort.

Each department within the organization as well as outside areas which interact with the organization should be considered for having a team member in the meeting. Those areas which have a significant stake in the problem should have a representative at the meeting. In my experience, problem solving teams are usually small (6 to 8 people) but they can be large in complex problems (18-20). Let's use a hypothetical example to illustrate a team which needs some great depth.

> Hypothetical problem: A critical plastic gear fails in operational use. In this case the part is purchased as a component and assembled into a gearbox which is furnished to an original equipment manufacturer for inclusion in a mechanical subsystem. Preliminary potential root causes are as follows:
>
> a) Improper molding resin

31

b) Improper molding conditions

c) Damage during assembly onto gear shaft

d) Chemical attack from lubrication oil in the gearbox

e) Assembly damage from the manufacturing operation at the manufacturing plant

f) The mechanical device design has changed and it is now loaded more than the original design intent of the gear.

g) Handling, shipping and storage through all phases, including the associated temperature and humidity effects.

h) In both the gearbox manufacturing operation and the customer's manufacturing operation, the process should be carefully evaluated for repair loops, requalification of rejects, customer returns, and any other loop which could put gears or gearboxes back into the system after initial assembly.

In the case above, how does anyone get all of the information needed to understand the problem, much less resolve it? The answer is that an *individual* is very unlikely to solve this problem. A team approach would look at each potential root cause and include a knowledgeable team member for each area of concern (a) through (g) above.

a) The material source expert may be the best team member to evaluate the adequacy of the molding resin.

b) Similarly the material source expert or a manufacturing engineer would be a good team member to evaluate the molding conditions.

c) A Manufacturing expert as well as a Manufacturing Engineering expert could best determine if the assembly onto the gear shaft could be a contributor.

d) Material experts, possibly from the material source could advise on the particular resin and its potential deterioration from the lubricating oil.

e) The customer (Plant Manufacturing Engineer) could work with the team to review the process of assembly and its potential to damage the gear.

f) The customer (Plant Design Engineer) can review the design change and its added load on the gear.

g) All Phases should evaluate their shipping, handling and storage as potential contributors to gear failure. This information could be given to the manufacturing engineer to bring to the team meeting.

h) Manufacturing loops of any kind are dangerous sources of problems. This should include (in this case) both the organization with the problem as well as the customer organization.

> This last item, manufacturing loops, is important enough to have a little more discussion. The examples are numerous but let me illustrate with an example of a repair loop. When the gearbox is manufactured, it is tested at the end of the line to see if it is ok to pack and ship. This testing involves many parameters. All failures are tossed or dropped into a reject bin. Later, at a slack time, an operator is given the task of either simply retesting the unit, repairing it, or else he may be instructed to disassemble it and save the good parts for future production. In this example, at least four negative things could happen (in reality there are many more bad things that could happen).

> 1. The plastic gear develops a hairline crack from the drop into the repair bin.

2.   Simply retesting the unit is an example of "Manufacturing Roulette." If this is the case in your operation there is a need to discourage this behavior in the strongest terms possible. This actually points to the need to make sure the tester's decision making ability meets the intended goal and the testers are set up equally. The author has personally seen the case where there were three testers at the end of the line and all rejects were retested through tester #3 which had the highest acceptance rate of the three testers.

3.   The person doing the retest and/or repair may be different each time, so there is no consistency to their method. In addition, off line operations are generally not watched closely so a person with poor training or poor attitude can do pretty much what he/she wants.

4. Disassembly is usually done with hand tools and by operators who are not fully trained or aware of the potential to damage parts. As parts are removed and inspected, they are put in "Good" or "Rejected" boxes for return to assembly. Such a system is a wide-open door for mixing of rejected parts with good parts.

Appendix VI – Methodology to develop Potential Root Causes.

Development of Potential *PROCESS* Root Causes
(See definition of process root cause in chapter 1)

Initially, go around the table and ask the first person to suggest a potential process root cause. Write it down on the flip chart and ask if you captured his/her idea adequately. Go to the next team members in succession. If someone wants to pass, that is ok and within the "everyone participates" rule.

When you get more passes than new ideas, ask the group for open discussion on potential process root causes. When someone tosses out an idea, ask them to give you time to write it down and verify that the written words capture his/her idea. When the open ideas session slows down, stop the brainstorming and tell the group if someone has a major item they want to add, they can do it later as long as it is in the team setting.

It is worth re-stating that any idea is ok. You will see that the value ideas surface during the prioritization step in the next chapter. If possible, encourage wild and crazy ideas as they tend to stimulate more imaginative contributions and this definitely breaks down barriers for timid people or those who worry that they will say something that will embarrass them.

As a side note, I once was working in England with a group of fuel system engineers on a fuel system design issue. One of the problems was associated with "Current Draw" or how much of the battery and/or generated power the fuel pump would use. One engineer suggested that the power source could be the fuel itself and there was no need for electrical circuitry to the pump. This was such a novel idea that I remember it clearly 30 years later. This engineer was a good engineer and he knew intuitively that this would not be a practical path to follow, but nevertheless, he threw out the idea. This suggestion started renewed imaginative thinking and a very good outcome resulted.

Appendix VII – Verification of Effectiveness of the Corrective Actions.

Once the team implements an action aimed at eliminating the root cause, the action plan must contain an evaluation of the process to determine the effectiveness of the corrective actions. This is a dual stage determination as follows:

1. Short Term: During the initial implementation of the corrective actions, each action should be tested to see if it can reliably do what the team thought it should do. One of the ways to do this in a manufacturing process is to present the known conditions which led to the process root cause and see if the new robust process can either detect it reliably or eliminate it. With non-manufacturing concerns, a similar plan must be developed to ensure the effectiveness of the fix.

2. Long term: This usually involves data collection and a monthly summary to be reviewed by the management. This step is usually achievable using readily available data such as (in the case of manufacturing) analysis of tester rejects, inspector reports, etc. It could also be expanded to include a view of customer rejections and warranty; however *there is a big caution here: Use of customer data or warranty data is not a main source of data for verification.* This is too late. It should be included along with data within your control as evidence of long-term satisfaction that we have truly eliminated the problem and not just masked it from our internal view.

With non-manufacturing problem analyses, there are similar tests that must be used to verify the effectiveness. With engineering issues, there are ES tests or special tests of durability, vibration, environment, etc. With Sales, Marketing, Purchasing, MP&L, and etc. similar tests have to be designed which essentially evaluate the system for preventing or at least catching concerns before they impact the organization.

Authors Notes:

How many times should we ask WHY?

In reality, the quest for "why" should stop when it gets to things totally out of anyone's control. For an oversimplified example, consider that we were working on the problem of "The picture fell off the wall hanger." If we asked "Why?" until we got down to GRAVITY, we are obviously wasting our time. This seems trivial, but there are many environmental factors which, if listed as root cause, which is out of our control and would not lead to a solution. Typically, we protect from such a cause rather than fix them. For example:

We buy a picture hanger rated for this specific picture

We make sure the wall is correct for the picture hanger

We make sure the picture hanger is installed correctly

The importance of a team effort

This can not be emphasized enough. It has been proven repeatedly that when people solve problems, the best individual effort is not as good as the worst effort by a proper team.

Formation of the team

The comments in section I (Use the Team Approach) cover this. However, here are some reinforcements that should be made.

Make a special effort to include people who want to work on the problem. Avoid those few people in the organization who are chronic complainers or otherwise have demonstrated an agenda not consistent with working within a team.

Who are the "Customers" in this issue?
Recognize that there are customers and suppliers within each organization. The Receiving Department is a Customer of both the supplier and the logistics firm. Additionally, the Receiving

Department is a supplier to the Manufacturing Floor. The Manufacturing floor is a supplier to the Shipping Department. This reciprocal relationship takes place within all organizations.

Guard against "Groupthink."

This is a phenomenon in which individuals feel the organizational pressure to an extent they are more focused on trying to please the boss or otherwise insecure about the political ramifications of saying what they think. Some organizations with powerful leaders who tend to be "Top-down" type of managers make sure that such people are excluded from the team. In this case, it would be a good idea to begin the meeting by talking about groupthink as a possible detriment. Everyone should be made to feel comfortable in expressing their ideas. This is more important when some people see flaws in the system or product but have been rebuked by their co-workers, supervisors, or managers when they try to discuss these issues.

Be a Bulldog on containment
One of the most common causes of a repeat problem is failure to contain. Everyone can easily see the obvious areas to perform containment:

> *The manufacturing operation*

> *The customer's Receiving Dock*

> *The customer's Manufacturing Floor*

There are, however many other considerations which could contain product which should be evaluated:

> *Stock which has been put on hold for other considerations*

> *Stock which is within a rework or repair process (Separate from the direct manufacturing operation)*

> *Parts in shipment*

Parts stored in distribution centers or warehouses, especially when these locations are at a remote location.

Customer returns for this reason or other reasons. (The "other reason" category is especially dangerous and must be evaluated).

"Show and Tell" parts which have been used for meetings, discussions or other illustrative purposes.

Use flipcharts during the group sessions:

It is the author's experience that nothing comes close to the large paper flip chart on an easel to gather the groups inputs. These are written real-time by the facilitator and remain displayed throughout the entire session. When a chart is full, DO NOT flip it over. Tear the chart from the pad and tape it on the wall of the conference room. Encourage team members to walk around and review the data on the charts as the process goes forward. This is especially important because it keeps all team members on the same page (literally.)

* * * * * * * * * * * * * * *

I hope you will find this book helpful. If you have recommendations for corrections or otherwise to improve it, please let me know.
mcpozz@gmail.com

Made in the USA
Columbia, SC
16 October 2020

22985998R00024